Animal Word Problems
Starring

Addition
and
Subtraction

Rebecca
Wingard-Nelson

Enslow Elementary, an imprint of Enslow Publishers, Inc.

Enslow Elementary® is a registered trademark of Enslow Publishers, Inc.

Library of Congress Cataloging-in-Publication Data

Wingard-Nelson, Rebecca.
  Animal word problems starring addition and subtraction : math word problems solved / Rebecca Wingard-Nelson.
      p. cm.   (Math word problems solved)
  Summary: "Explores methods of solving addition and subtraction word problems using animal examples" Provided by publisher.
  Includes bibliographical references and index.
  ISBN-13: 978-0-7660-2917-0
  ISBN-10: 0-7660-2917-4
  1. Addition—Juvenile literature. 2. Subtraction—Juvenile literature.
  3. Animals—Juvenile literature. I. Title.
  QA115.W7524 2009
  513.2'11—dc22
                                        2007051780

Printed in the United States of America

10 9 8 7 6 5 4 3 2 1

To Our Readers: We have done our best to make sure all Internet Addresses in this book were active and appropriate when we went to press. However, the author and the publisher have no control over and assume no liability for the material available on those Internet sites or on other Web sites they may link to. Any comments or suggestions can be sent by e-mail to comments@enslow.com or to the address on the back cover.

♻ Enslow Publishers, Inc., is committed to printing our books on recycled paper. The paper in every book contains 10% to 30% post-consumer waste (PCW). The cover board on the outside of each book contains 100% PCW. Our goal is to do our part to help young people and the environment too!

Illustrations: Tom LaBaff

Cover illustration: Tom LaBaff

Free Worksheets are available for this book at http://www.enslow.com. Search for the **Math Word Problems Solved** series name. The publisher will provide access to the worksheets for five years from the book's first publication date.

Contents

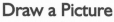

Introduction

"Why do I have to do math?"

> Math is used in your life every day.
> Word problems show you some of the ways.

"But I hate word problems."

> But you use word problems all the time, and you
> probably don't even realize it.

"The stories in word problems would never happen!"

> Sometimes math word problems don't look very real.
> A lot of real-life word problems are very hard to solve.
> For now, have fun getting started on word problems
> about animals.

"How can this book help me?"

> This book will give you helpful tips for solving a
> word problem. Learn how to understand the
> question, how to plan a way to solve it, and how to
> check your answer. You'll see that word problems
> really are "no problem" after all!

Problem-Solving Tips

Word problems might be part of your homework, on a test, or in your life. These tips can help you solve them, no matter where they show up.

 Be positive!
When you get a problem right the first time, good for you! When you don't get a problem right the first time, but you learn from your mistakes, AWESOME for you! You learned something new!

 Get help early!
New problems build on old ones. If you don't understand today's problem, tomorrow's problem will be even harder to understand.

 Do your homework!
The more you practice anything, the better you become at it. You can't play an instrument or play a sport well without practice. Homework problems are your practice.

 Move on!
If you get stuck, move to the next problem. Do the ones you know how to solve first. You'll feel more confident. And you won't miss the ones you know because you ran out of time. Go back later and try the problems you skipped.

Ask questions!

When someone is helping you, asking good questions tells the person what you don't understand. If you don't ask questions, you will never get answers!

Take a break!

If you have tried everything you can think of but are only getting frustrated, take a break. Close your eyes and take a deep breath. Stretch your arms and legs. Get a drink of water or a snack. Then come back and try again.

Don't give up!

The first time you try to solve a word problem, you might come up with an answer that does not make sense, or that you know is not right. Don't give up! Check your math. Try solving the problem a different way. If you quit, you won't learn.

In some problems, you will see clue spotters. A magnifying glass will help you spy clue words in the problem.

Problem-Solving Steps

Word problems can be solved by following four easy steps.

Here's the problem.

One kind of stickleback fish has five spines on its back. Another kind of stickleback has three. If the fish swim together, how many spines are there in all?

① Read and understand the problem.

Read the problem carefully.
Put the problem in your own words.

What do you know?
One stickleback has five spines.
One stickleback has three spines.

What are you trying to find?
The number of spines the fish have together.

To understand the problem, ask yourself other questions, like:
What is happening in the problem? Are there any clue words? Have I ever seen a problem like this one?

② Make a plan.

Some problems tell you what plan to use, like make a table or draw a picture. For other problems, you make your own plan. Use whatever plan makes the most sense and is easiest for you. Some plans you might try are:

Look for a pattern.   Write an equation.
Estimate.   Use a model.
Guess and check.   Break it apart.

How can you solve this problem?
You can write an equation to add the number of spines on each fish together.

9

③ Solve the problem.

It is time to do the math!
If you find that your plan
is not working, make a
new plan. Don't give up the
first time. Write your answer.
Make sure you include the units.

Let's write an equation.
One stickleback has 5 spines, the other has 3
spines. Add 5 + 3.

$$5 + 3 = 8$$

**If the two fish swim together, there are
8 spines in all.**

④ Look back.

The problem is solved!
But you aren't finished yet.
Take a good look at your answer.
Does it make sense? Did you include the
units? Did you use the right numbers to
begin? Estimate or use a different operation to
check your math. Is there another plan you
could have used to solve the problem?

Does the answer make sense?
Yes.

Is the math correct?
Yes, 5 + 3 = 8.

Is there another way to solve the problem?
Yes, you can draw a picture and count the spines.

Try the other plan and see if you get the same answer.
You can count 8 spines on the two fish. Either plan gives the same answer, 8 spines.

Equations

An equation is a sentence that uses numbers.

Here's the problem.

An inchworm took 3 hours to crawl up a tree. It took 2 more hours to crawl along a branch to a leaf. In all, how long did it take the inchworm to reach the leaf? Write an equation to show how long it took.

ADDITION

Read and understand.
What do you know?
The inchworm took 3 hours to crawl up the tree.
It took 2 hours to crawl along the branch.

What are you trying to find?
How long it took the inchworm to reach the leaf.

Plan.
The problem tells us to find the answer, then
write an equation to show what happened.
Let's find the answer by counting on.

Solve.
The inchworm took 3 hours to crawl up the tree.
Start at 3. It took 2 more hours to crawl along
the branch.

Start at 3, then count two more: 4, 5.

**It took the inchworm 5 hours in all to reach
the leaf.**

Now, write the equation.
Think about the whole story.

3 hours up tree + 2 hours along branch = 5 hours

3 + 2 = 5

Look back.
Does the answer make sense? Yes.
Did you answer the right question? Yes.

Is This Addition?

? Here's the problem. ?

**Mia has geckos living in her garden.
There are 5 types of geckos that are
active at night. There are 2 other
types of geckos that are active during
the day. How many types of geckos
are in Mia's garden in total?**

ADDITION

 Read and understand.
What do you know?
Mia has 5 types of night geckos in her garden.
She also has 2 types of day geckos.

What are you trying to find?
How many types of geckos are in Mia's garden.

Are there any clue words in the problem?
Clue words are words that tell you what kind of
equation you can write to solve the problem.
Here are some clue words that tell you when a
problem uses addition: add, combined, sum,
total, plus, in all, together, increase, both.

This problem uses the clue word "total."
It is an addition problem.

Problems that combine groups, such as night geckos and day geckos, are addition problems.

Plan.
Let's write an addition equation.

Solve.
Write an equation that uses the numbers from the problem.

$$
\begin{array}{r}
5 \text{ types of night geckos} \\
+\ 2 \text{ types of day geckos} \\
\hline
7 \text{ types of geckos total}
\end{array}
$$

Mia has 7 types of geckos in her garden.

Look back.
Does the answer make sense? Yes.

Is the math correct?
Yes, $5 + 2 = 7$.

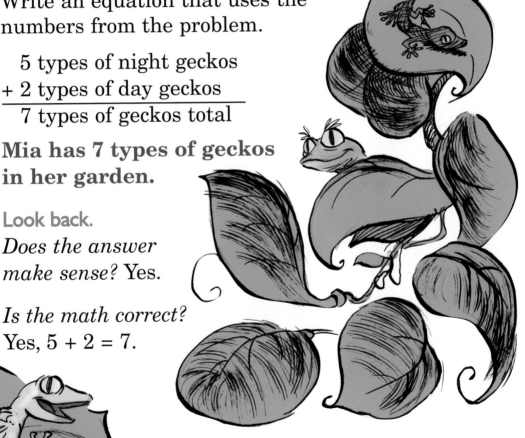

Is This Subtraction?

How can you tell if a word problem
is a subtraction problem?

Here's the problem.

Two toucans tossed 8 red berries
and 6 yellow berries back and
forth to each other. How many more
red berries did they toss than
yellow berries?

Read and understand.
What do you know?
The toucans tossed 8 red berries.
The toucans tossed 6 yellow berries.

What are you trying to find?
How many more red berries were tossed than
yellow berries.

Are there any clue words in the problem?
Here are some clue words that tell you when a
problem uses subtraction: subtract, difference,
take away, how much less, how many more,
remain, left, fewer.

This problem uses the clue words "how many more."
It is a subtraction problem.

Problems that find the difference between two amounts are subtraction problems.

Plan.

Let's write a subtraction equation.

Solve.

To find the difference between two amounts, begin with the larger value and subtract the smaller value. Begin with the number of red berries, 8. Subtract the number of yellow berries, 6.

$8 - 6 = 2$

The toucans tossed 2 more red berries than they did yellow berries.

Look back.

Is the math correct?
Yes, $8 - 6 = 2$.

When boy and girl toucans toss berries back and forth they are saying, "I really like you."

Inverse Operations

Addition and subtraction are inverse operations.
They do the opposite of each other.
You can use inverse operations to check your answers.

? Here's the problem.

Manny has 9 tarantulas. When he woke up, only 2 were in the cage. How many tarantulas had escaped?

Read and understand.

What do you know?
Manny has 9 tarantulas.
2 were in the cage.

What are you trying to find?
The number of tarantulas that had escaped.

What kind of problem is this?
There were some tarantulas, then some went away. This is subtraction.

Plan.
Write a subtraction equation.

Solve.

```
  9 tarantulas
− 2 tarantulas in cage
  7 tarantulas escaped
```

There were 7 tarantulas that escaped.

Look back.
You can check the answer to a subtraction problem by using addition.
Add the answer (7) to the number you subtracted (2). $7 + 2 = 9$
If the sum (9) is the number you started with, then your answer is correct.
Did you start with 9? Yes.

Do I Have Enough Information?

When you do not have enough information,
you cannot solve a word problem.

Here's the problem.

Ring-tailed lemurs are about
18 inches long. Their bushy tails
are longer than their bodies. There
are 23 black and white rings on their
tails. About how much longer
is a ring-tailed lemur's tail than
its body?

SUBTRACTION

Read and understand.
The lemur's body is about 18 inches long.
Its tail is longer than its body.
Its tail has 23 rings.

Plan.
The clue words "how much longer" tell you this
is a subtraction problem. Subtract the length of
the lemur's body from the length of its tail.

Solve.
There is not enough information. The problem
does not tell you how long the tail is.

Read the problem again. Was the information given, and you just missed it? No, the problem says the lemur's tail is longer than its body, but it does not tell you how long the tail is. There is not enough information to solve the problem.

21

I Have Too Much Information!

Some problems give more information than you need. This can be confusing!

Here's the problem.

Some hens, like Rhode Island Reds and Orpingtons, lay brown eggs. Leghorn hens lay white eggs. The McMurray family has <u>6 Rhode Island Red</u> hens, <u>4 Orpington</u> hens, and <u>10 Leghorn</u> hens. They also have <u>9 Araucana</u> hens that lay blue eggs. How many hens do they have that lay brown eggs in all?

ADDITION

22

Read and understand.

What do you know?

Underline the types of hens in the problem so that you don't miss any. Sort what you know by making a chart of the hens, how many of each, and what color eggs they lay.

Type	Number	Egg color
Rhode Island Red	6	brown
Orpington	4	brown
Leghorn	10	white
Araucana	9	blue

What are you trying to find?

The number of hens that lay brown eggs.

Plan.

Let's add only the hens that lay brown eggs.

Solve.

$$
\begin{array}{r}
6 \text{ Rhode Island Red hens} \\
+\ 4 \text{ Orpington hens} \\
\hline
10 \text{ hens that lay brown eggs}
\end{array}
$$

The McMurrays have 10 hens that lay brown eggs.

Look back.

Did you use the right information? Yes.

Does your answer match the problem? Yes.

Draw a Picture

A picture can help you find the answer to a problem.

? ?

Here's the problem.

An orangutan picked 9 mangos. It threw 3 of the mangos into the bushes. How many were left?

Read and understand.
What do you know?
The orangutan picked 9 mangos.
It threw 3 away.

What are you trying to find?
The number of mangos that were left.

Plan.
Let's draw a picture to solve the problem.

Solve.
Your picture does not need to be perfect.
You can use circles to show the mangos.

Draw a picture to show the
9 mangos that were picked.

Cross off the 3 mangos
that were thrown away.

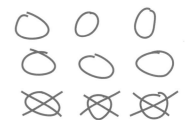

Count the mangos that are left in the picture.
There are 6.

There are 6 orangutans? NO! There are 6
mangos. Make sure you tell the whole answer.

There were 6 mangos left.

 Look back.

Does the answer make sense? Yes.

Have you seen problems like this before?
Yes, this problem had some
things (mangos), then
some went away.

*What kind of problem
is this?*
It is a subtraction
problem.

25

Zeros

Some problems are easy to solve when you know about zeros.

? Here's the problem. ?

An opossum ate 27 grubs in the morning. It did not eat any grubs in the afternoon. How many grubs did it eat in all?

ADDITION

Read and understand.
What do you know?
The opossum ate 27 grubs in the morning.
It ate zero more in the afternoon.

What are you trying to find?
The number of grubs the opossum ate in all.

Plan.
Since the opossum ate zero grubs in the afternoon, you can use what you know about zeros to answer the question.

Solve.
When you add or subtract a zero, the original number does not change.

The opossum ate 27 grubs in the morning and zero more in the afternoon. Zero is nothing, so in all the opossum ate only the 27 grubs from the morning.

The opossum ate 27 grubs in all.

When opossums feel threatened, they often stick out their tongues and pretend to be dead.

 Look back.

Does the answer make sense? Yes.
Did you include the units in the answer? Yes.

MMMM!

More Zeros

When you take away everything, zero is always left.

Here's the problem.

Eight ducks were all quacking at a dog. The dog barked. Eight ducks ran away. How many ducks were left?

SUBTRACTION

 Read and understand.
What do you know?
There were 8 ducks. They were all quacking. All 8 ducks ran away.

What are you trying to find?
The number of ducks left.

Is there anything special about this problem?
Yes, the numbers are the same. All 8 ducks ran away.

 Plan.
Let's use what you know about zeros.

 Solve.
When you take away the same number you start with, the answer is always zero.

We started with 8 ducks. All 8 of them ran away.
There were none, or zero, left.
There are no ducks left.

 Look back.

Does the answer make sense? Yes.
Use an equation to check your work.
$8 - 8 = 0$

Place-Value Drawings

When the numbers in the problem have more than one digit, it can help you to make a place-value drawing.

Here's the problem.

Under a bridge, 124 small brown bats sleep during the day. Another 132 bats sleep in a nearby barn. Combined, how many bats sleep under the bridge and in the barn?

 Read and understand.
What do you know?
124 bats are sleeping under the bridge.
132 bats are sleeping in the barn.

What are you trying to find?
The number of bats in all.

Plan.

This problem uses three-digit numbers.
Let's use a place-value drawing.

A place-value drawing uses dots
for digits in the ones place.

Ten dots joined together form a
line for a digit in the tens place.

100   10 1

Ten lines joined together form
a box for a digit in the hundreds place.

Solve.

Using a place-value drawing,
draw 124 for the bats under
the bridge.

124

Now draw 132 for the bats in
the barn.

132

Use the place-value drawing to
count how many bats in all.
Count the total in each place.

Begin in the ones place.
There are 6 ones.   6
There are 5 tens.   56
There are 2 hundreds.   256

There are 256 bats in all.

Look back.

Did you start with the right numbers? Yes.

Grouping Addition

Sometimes when you add numbers, the total in one place will group into the next larger place.

Here's the problem.

There were 28 blue dragonflies sitting on a pond. There were 7 green dragonflies on the same pond. In all, how many dragonflies were on the pond?

Read and understand.
What do you know?
There were 28 blue dragonflies.
There were 7 green dragonflies.

What are you trying to find?
The number of dragonflies in all.

Plan.
Let's use a place-value drawing.

Solve.
There were 28 blue dragonflies.
Draw 28 using a place-value drawing.

28

Now draw the 7 more dragonflies.
that landed.

28 + 7

Ten dots can be grouped into a line.
Circle 10 ones dots.
Cross out the circle, and draw a ten-line.

Use the place-value drawing to count
how many dragonflies in all.
There are 3 tens. There are 5 ones.

3 tens   5 ones

35

28 + 7 = 35
In all, there were 35 dragonflies on the pond.

Look back.
Does the answer match the question? Yes.
Did you start with the right numbers? Yes.

Grouping Subtraction

Sometimes when you subtract, you need to break a group from one place value into smaller units.

There are more than 20 kinds of armadillos, but only one kind can roll up into a ball.

? Here's the problem.

Twenty armadillos were resting in the sun. A coyote scared them, and five of them rolled up into balls. How many did not roll up into a ball?

Read and understand.
What do you know?
There were 20 armadillos.
Five rolled up into balls.

What are you trying to find?
How many armadillos did not roll up into a ball.

Plan.
Let's use a place-value drawing.

Solve.
There are 20 armadillos.
Draw 20 using a place-value drawing.

Five of them rolled into balls. Five is in the ones
place, but there are no ones in 20.

One ten is the same as ten ones.
Replace one ten with ten ones.

Cross off five ones for the five armadillos
that rolled into balls. Count how many
are left. There are fifteen.

$20 - 5 = 15$
Fifteen armadillos did not roll up into a ball.

Look back.
Does the answer make sense? Yes.
Does the answer match the question? Yes.

Mental Addition

When numbers end in zeros, you can add or subtract them in your head.

Here's the problem.

Each hedgehog has about 7,000 quills, or hollow hairs. About how many quills do two hedgehogs have together?

Read and understand.
What do you know?
One hedgehog has about 7,000 quills.

What are you trying to find?
The number of quills on two hedgehogs together.

Plan.
Let's use mental math to add the number of quills.

Solve.
7,000 + 7,000
Think:
There are no ones, tens, or hundreds. I only need to add the digits in the thousands place.

7 + 7 = 14, so 7,000 + 7,000 = 14,000

Two hedgehogs together have about 14,000 quills.

Look back.

Did you remember to include the units in your answer? Yes.

Is your math correct?
Yes, 7,000 + 7,000 = 14,000.

Mental Subtraction

You can subtract mentally by using place value.

Here's the problem.

There were 200 electric eels living on a reef. A science team carefully collected 112 of the eels to study. How many eels were left on the reef?

SUBTRACTION

Read and understand.

What do you know?
There were 200 eels on the reef.
A team took 112 of the eels.

What are you trying to find?
The number of eels left on the reef.

Are there any clue words?
Yes, the clue word "left" tells you to use subtraction.

Plan.

Let's use mental math to subtract.

Solve.

200 – 112

You can subtract in your head by thinking of 112
as 100 + 10 + 2, and subtracting in steps.

Start with 200 and subtract the hundreds, 100.
200 – 100 = 100

From what is left, 100, subtract the tens, 10.
100 – 10 = 90

From what is left, 90, subtract the ones, 2.
90 – 2 = 88

200 – 112 = 88
There were 88 electric eels left on the reef.

Look back.

*Did you remember to include the units in your
answer?* Yes.

More Addition Equations

You can use equations to help you add numbers with more than one digit.

Here's the problem.

The elephant seal and the sea lion are both kinds of seals. There are 128 elephant seals on a beach. There are also 263 sea lions on the beach. How many seals are on the beach?

Read and understand.
What do you know?
There are 128 elephant seals.
There are 263 sea lions.
Elephant seals and sea lions are seals.

What are you trying to find?
The number of seals.

What kind of problem is this?
There are no clue words, but to find the number of seals, you must combine the elephant seals and sea lions. It is an addition problem.

Plan.
Write an addition equation.

40

Solve.

128 elephant seals + 263 seal lions = total seals

$$128 + 263 = \underline{\hspace{1cm}}$$

Numbers with more than one digit are easier to add when you write them in columns to line up the place values.

Add the ones place.	Add the tens place.	Add the hundreds place.
8 + 3 = 11	1 + 2 + 6 = 9	1 + 2 = 3

$$\begin{array}{r} \overset{1}{1}28 \\ +\ 263 \\ \hline 1 \end{array}$$ Group 11 as 1 ten and 1 one.

$$\begin{array}{r} \overset{1}{1}28 \\ +\ 263 \\ \hline 91 \end{array}$$

$$\begin{array}{r} \overset{1}{1}28 \\ +\ 263 \\ \hline 391 \end{array}$$

There are 391 seals on the beach.

 Look back.

Did you answer the right question? Yes.

More Subtraction Equations

You can write subtraction equations to help you subtract numbers with more than one digit.

Here's the problem.

An aquarium has 140 jellyfish and 34 squid. How many more jellyfish are there than squid?

SUBTRACTION

Read and understand.

What do you know?
There are 140 jellyfish.
There are 34 squid.

What are you trying to find?
The difference between the number of jellyfish and the number of squid.

Are there any clue words?
Yes, the words "how many more" tell you this is a subtraction problem.

Plan.
Write a subtraction equation.

Solve.
140 – 34 = _____

Jellyfish have no bones, no heart, no eyes, no ears, and no brain!

Write the numbers in columns to line up the place values.

Subtract ones.
You cannot subtract 4 from 0.
Remember, 1 ten is the same as 10 ones. Take 1 ten and group it as 10 ones. $10 - 4 = 6$

$$\begin{array}{r} {}^{3}\ {}^{10} \\ 1\cancel{4}0 \\ -\ \ 34 \\ \hline 6 \end{array}$$

Subtract tens. $3 - 3 = 0$
There are no hundreds to subtract, so bring down the 1.

$$\begin{array}{r} {}^{3}\ {}^{10} \\ 1\cancel{4}0 \\ -\ \ 34 \\ \hline 106 \end{array}$$

There are 106 more jellyfish than squid.

 Look back.

Does the answer make sense? Yes.
Is the math correct? Check your subtraction by adding. $106 + 34 = 140$. Good!

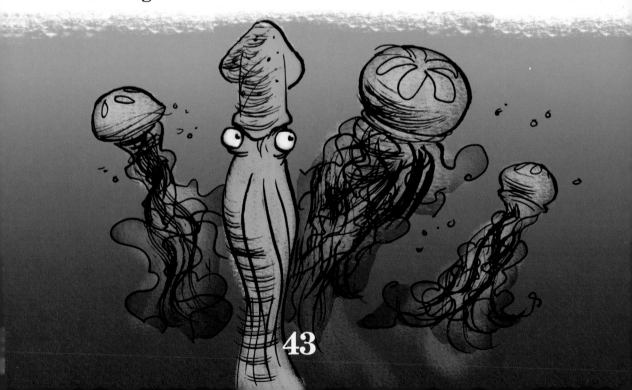

Estimation

You can use estimation when you do not need to know the exact answer to a problem.

? Here's the problem.

A bison rancher has 189 bison in a corral. He has 214 bison in a large pasture and 176 more in a small pasture. About how many bison does the rancher have in total?

 Read and understand.
What do you know?
There are 189 bison in the corral.
There are 214 bison in the large pasture.
There are 176 bison in the small pasture.

Is there anything special about this problem?
Yes. The problem asks "about how many."
The answer does not need to be exact.

What are you trying to find?
An estimate of the total number of bison.

 Plan.
Let's estimate the answer by rounding each number to the greatest place value, the hundreds place.

44

Solve.

Round each number to the hundreds place.	Add the rounded numbers.

189 rounds to 200   200

214 rounds to 200   200

176 rounds to 200   + 200

                                     600

The rancher has about 600 bison.

Look back.

Does the answer make sense? Yes.

Did you answer the right question? Yes.

Let's Review

To solve a word problem follow these steps:

Read and understand the problem.
Know what the problem says, and what you need to find. If you don't understand, ask questions before you start.

Make a plan.
Choose the plan that makes the most sense and is easiest for you. Remember, there is usually more than one way to find the right answer.

Solve the problem.
Use the plan. If your first plan isn't working, try a different one. Take a break and come back with a fresh mind.

Look Back.
Read the problem again. Make sure your answer makes sense. Check your math. If the answer does not look right, don't give up now! Use what you've learned to go back and try the problem again.

Further Reading

Adler, David A. *You Can, Toucan, Math: Word Problem–Solving Fun.* New York: Holiday House, 2006.

Murphy, Stuart J. *Coyotes All Around.* New York: HarperTrophy, 2003.

Scieszka, Jon. *Math Curse.* New York: Viking, 2007.

Internet Addresses

Aplusmath
<http://www.aplusmath.com>

Math Playground
<http://www.mathplayground.com/word problems.html>

Coolmath Games
<http://www.coolmath-games.com>

Index